Acts
Leader Guide

Acts
Catching Up with the Spirit

Acts
978-1-5018-9455-8
978-1-5018-9456-5 eBook

Acts DVD
978-1-5018-9459-6

Acts Leader Guide
978-1-5018-9457-2
978-1-5018-9458-9 eBook

MATTHEW L. SKINNER

ACTS

CATCHING UP WITH THE SPIRIT

LEADER GUIDE

BY MIKE S. POTEET

Abingdon Press / Nashville

Acts
Leader Guide

CONTENTS

Introduction 7

Session 1: What God Has Done 10

Session 2: What God Does 19

Session 3: Discernment and Change 26

Session 4: Opposition 36

Session 5: Saints around the Edges 45

Session 6: This Changes Everything 55

INTRODUCTION

In *Acts: Catching Up with the Spirit*, Dr. Matthew Skinner encourages Christians to read large portions of the Acts of the Apostles in order to discover how the book, in his words, "has a way of igniting our imaginations."

For Skinner, Acts asks more questions than it answers, prodding readers to wrestle in deeper and more fruitful ways with who Jesus is, what it means to be Jesus' church, and how best to engage with and influence the wider world as Jesus' witnesses.

Skinner emphasizes the Holy Spirit in his book's title because in Acts, "the main way Jesus is present and active is through the Holy Spirit." Far from being *"the history of the first Christians,"* Acts is the story—often a wild and strange one—of how "Jesus Christ, active through the Holy Spirit, [is] continuing his work of liberating people from all kinds of oppression and alienation."

This Leader Guide presents outlines and activity plans for six sessions that groups can use to explore the themes Skinner highlights in Acts. The sessions include readings and discussions of many of the same stories (or portions of them) that Skinner presents in his book. You and your group will get the most value from this Leader Guide when you use it alongside *Acts: Catching Up with the Spirit*. A six-session DVD featuring Skinner is also available to enhance each session of your study.

The following list describes the six sessions for the leader to facilitate in this study:

- **"Session 1: What God Has Done"** helps participants appreciate how Acts defines the Christian message and evaluate how Acts' presentation of the good news can inform their own.

- **"Session 2: What God Does"** encourages participants to connect their own experiences of inclusion and exclusion with the Spirit's broad inclusion of strangers and outsiders, and to find ways, as the earliest Christians had to find ways, to follow the Spirit's lead.

- **"Session 3: Discernment and Change"** prompts participants to consider the similarities and differences between decision-making and discernment, and to examine how the early church sought to clarify its understanding of God's activity in the world.

- **"Session 4: Opposition"** invites participants to reconsider opposition to the church, both in Acts and in the present day, as opportunities for the church to grow in its understanding of its identity, witness, and work.

- **"Session 5: Saints around the Edges"** asks participants to examine how several of Acts' "supporting characters" offer relevant insights into serving God today, and to offer thanks for individuals in their own congregations and lives who make unique contributions to the church's witness.

- **"Session 6: This Changes Everything"** challenges participants to examine some practical political and economic implications of the good news in Acts' world and in our own.

Introduction

As you prepare to lead these sessions, you will want to do the following:

- Carefully read the chapter of *Acts: Catching Up with the Spirit* corresponding to each session. Note anything you find confusing or about which you have further questions, and consult trusted biblical resources (study Bibles, commentaries, and so forth) for more information.

- Arrange a comfortable and physically accessible meeting space for all participants.

- Provide Bibles for participants who do not bring their own, a markerboard or large sheets of paper and markers, and nametags (optional). Most sessions do not call for extra materials.

Unless noted otherwise, all Scripture quotations are from the New Revised Standard Version Bible.

May this guide help you and your group discover the Holy Spirit's continuing power to use the Acts of the Apostles to spur Christ's church toward more faithful living and bolder witness to God's saving presence.

Session 1

WHAT GOD HAS DONE

SESSION OBJECTIVES

This session's Bible readings, discussion, reflection, and prayer will equip participants to

- appreciate the nature and purpose of the Acts of the Apostles;
- closely examine passages from Acts for definitions of the Christian message and statements of its significance; and
- consider where and how Christians today, as communities and individuals, can witness in word and in deed to God's activity.

VIDEO SEGMENT

- On the *Acts: Catching Up with the Spirit* DVD, watch the video segment for Session 1 prior to the session. Prepare a question or two to be used for discussion.

- Decide when the participants will view the video during this session, whether at the beginning of the session, before or after a discussion time, or toward the end of the session. Allow 15 minutes to watch and discuss the video.

- Prepare the means to show the video to the group.

SESSION I OPENING DISCUSSION

Welcome the participants. Express your enthusiasm for studying *Acts: Catching Up with the Spirit* with them. Tell them about your own interest in leading the study, and invite volunteers to talk briefly about why they are interested in taking part.

Tell participants that Matthew Skinner, in his Preface, calls Acts one of the New Testament's "more neglected writings." Ask participants whether they agree with this assessment of Acts, and why. Then ask them to tell you, without opening a Bible, what they remember, know, or think they know about the Book of Acts. Write a list of their responses on the markerboard or large sheets of paper.

Read aloud from Skinner's Introduction:

> Acts describes episodes and people from the young church's history so that communities of believers near the end of the first century would know who they were. Acts tells its stories so Christians would remember what God had called them to do and how God had been faithful so far.

Discuss:

- When and how have stories about the past helped you strengthen your sense of identity and purpose in the present?

- How are telling and hearing these kinds of identity-shaping, purpose-affirming stories like and unlike studying history?

- How do we know if and when the stories we rely on for identity and purpose need to be told in different ways—or exchanged for different stories?

11

Tell participants this study seeks to understand how and why the stories in Acts have helped the Christian church remember its identity and purpose for two thousand years, and how Acts can, as Skinner writes in his Preface, "inspire us to consider anew what Christian faith and life should look like in our complicated age."

OPENING PRAYER

Holy God of power and purpose, your Spirit swept over the waters at Creation and is sweeping through the world even today. During this time of study, may we feel your Spirit stir around and within us in fresh ways, that we may be strengthened to respond as faithful followers of him on whom your Spirit rested in a special way, our Savior and Lord, Jesus Christ. Amen.

BIBLE READING AND DISCUSSION

Have participants turn in their Bible to Acts 1. Tell participants that Acts is a continuation of or "sequel" to the Gospel of Luke, written by the same author to the same audience: "Theophilus," who may have been an individual patron or who could represent any believer reading the book; the name *Theophilus* means "lover of God."

Recruit one or more volunteers to read **Acts 1:1-11** aloud. (You may want to have different readers read the parts of the narrator, Jesus, Jesus' followers, and the men in white robes.)

Discuss the reading using some or all of these questions:

- What expectations does this first story in Acts raise for the whole book?

- Matthew Skinner says the phrase in the first verse describing the contents of Luke's Gospel (his "first scroll") is best translated "all that Jesus began to do and teach," and that this translation frames all that follows as an account of Jesus' "remain[ing] active in the world" through the church. How does thinking about the church as a way Jesus is active in the world affect your attitudes toward it? In your own experience, what about the church supports this idea? What challenges it?

- What does this story tell us about Jesus? What does it tell us about the Holy Spirit, and why the Spirit matters to Jesus' followers? Why do you think Jesus describes the Spirit's imminent arrival as a baptism?

- "Christian 'witness' is at the heart of believers' activity in Acts," writes Skinner. What does being a "witness" mean? Do you find the idea of being a "witness" to Jesus intimidating? exhilarating? something in between, or something else altogether? Why?

- Who are the men in white robes who appear to Jesus' followers? What is their connection, if any, to the men who appear to the women at Jesus' tomb in **Luke 24:1-12?**

Read aloud this quotation from *Acts: Catching Up with the Spirit*: "[Jesus' followers] are going to spread the Christian message. . . . What are they going to tell people? What exactly has God done? What is this new Christian message, after all?"

Form three small teams of participants and assign to each team one of the following Scriptures to read and discuss. Tell participants these passages are excerpted from a longer passage Skinner discusses, and encourage them to pay attention in their discussions to their assigned verses' context.

Ask teams to pretend, for this activity, that their assigned passage and its immediate context contain the only information they have about the Christian message. Encourage teams to glean from each passage all they can about what that message is and why it matters. (You may want or need to assure participants there will be time to discuss all three passages together after the exercise.)

You may wish to copy and distribute to teams the questions following each passage as additional discussion prompts, or use them as aids to your whole group discussion later in this session.

Acts 2:22-33

- The crowd of "fellow Israelites" Peter addresses is ethnically and culturally diverse (see 2:5-11). Skinner notes: "[V]ariation is one of the church's original characteristics. The church of Jesus Christ consists of a unity that gathers differences and distinctions into a common home. That's a message many congregations I know need to hear." Does your congregation need to hear it? Why or why not?

- In 2:16-21, Peter interprets the Holy Spirit's arrival and the resulting miracle of languages as evidence of "the last days," which Skinner defines as "a new culminating chapter in God's history with the world." What does the story of the first Christian Pentecost show Christians doing during "the last days"? How does or how should this story shape Christian interest today in "the last days"?

- What does Jesus' resurrection prove about him, according to Peter?

- Peter goes on, in 2:37-40, to call on people to "repent"—as Skinner writes, "to change their minds about Jesus"—and be baptized. When, in your own or others' experience, have you seen a proclamation

of the Christian message inspire repentance? Should
all presentations of the message seek to inspire repentance? Why or why not?

Acts 3:12-26

- Skinner notes Peter's speech is followed by "the first
  healing performed by apostles" in Acts (see 3:1-10).
  Miracles in the Bible usually point to something
  beyond themselves. What is this miraculous healing's
  significance, according to Peter?

- Peter says the people and their leaders "acted in ignorance" when rejecting and crucifying Jesus. Why does
  he still call on them to change their "hearts and lives"
  (verse 19 CEB) in response to the Christian message?
  How much, if at all, does ignorance excuse sin?

- Peter says God has promised "the restoration of all
  things" (verse 21 CEB). Pointing out that Peter
  doesn't describe what he means in detail, Skinner
  writes, "Maybe the point of the ambiguity is to
  call our imaginations into action." What does your
  reading of the Bible lead you to imagine "the restoration of all things" will be like? What are you doing
  (or could you be doing) now to anticipate this
  universal restoration?

Acts 17:22-31

- Skinner calls this passage "a trophy story" because "in
  Athens, the place that symbolizes the intellectual accom-
  plishments of the ancient Greek-speaking world,"
  Paul spoke and the Athenians listened. What specific
  places or types of places are the equivalent of ancient
  Athens in the world today? How would you or how
  do you present the Christian message in these places?

- Would you characterize Paul's proclamation of the Christian message in Athens as successful? Why or why not? What is the difference, if any, between being a successful witness to Jesus and being a faithful one?

- What lessons about presenting the Christian message to nonbelievers today do you think Christians, as individuals and as the church, can learn from Paul's example?

After allowing sufficient time for teams to discuss their assigned passages, bring the whole group together. Ask each team to report highlights from their discussions. Then lead a broader discussion using some or all of these questions:

- What major similarities do you notice among how these passages define the Christian message? What major differences, if any, do you notice, and how do you understand those differences?

- What response or responses to the Christian message do these passages call for? How relevant are these responses today, and why?

- How do these passages show Jesus as both consistent with and different from God's past history with the people of Israel? Why is it important for Christians today to remember that, as Skinner writes, "[t]he Christian message derives from older Jewish convictions and hopes"? What implications does this remembrance have for how Christians should relate to Jews today?

- Reflecting on Acts 17, Skinner writes, "I don't think anyone can *prove* that Jesus was raised from the dead. That piece of Christian faith depends not on the tools of science, history, philosophy, or militaries but on the witness of the entire church." In what specific ways has the church's witness shaped your faith? Which congregations or organizations, and which specific believers, have influenced your belief in the risen Christ?

- Skinner points out these passages are mostly speeches, but "speeches are not the only way Acts communicates what the good news is and what changes it sets in motion." How do you know when speech is or is not required for you to be a witness to Jesus?

PLAN TO TAKE ACTION

Read aloud from Matthew Skinner:

> The entire narrative of Acts, through its stories about speeches, events, struggles, and discoveries, reaffirms the belief that God has acted and continues to act.

Tell participants that each session in this study of Acts will end with an opportunity for them to commit to taking some concrete action of their own as a faithful response to God's action.

Refer participants to the story Skinner tells in chapter 1 of his book about being a witness to a car accident, emphasizing the police officer's instruction to him: "You can only tell me what you saw." Suggest that this session's stories from Acts show us that our primary responsibility as witnesses to Jesus is to tell other people how we have seen God at work—in the world, and in our own lives.

Allow participants a few minutes to think about and reflect on one specific way they believe they have seen God at work. Then instruct participants to form small groups of two or

17

three and practice telling each other about that glimpse of God's activity. Encourage participants to be sincere, direct, and succinct. Tell them not to judge each other, but simply listen to each other. No participant should be pressured or shamed into talking about their response.

CLOSING PRAYER

After all small group members who wish to have practiced their witness, lead a time of silent closing prayer, using these two questions as prompts:

- To whom may God be calling you to talk this week about what you have seen God do?

- What actions may God be calling you to take this week to show why what God has done matters to you?

Session 2

WHAT GOD DOES

SESSION OBJECTIVES

This session's Bible readings, discussion, reflection, and prayer will equip participants to

- reflect on their experiences of being strangers and outsiders to others;
- discover how "conversion stories" in Acts confirm or challenge their understanding of "conversion"; and
- identify people outside their faith community whom God may be calling them to welcome, include, and commit themselves to.

VIDEO SEGMENT

- On the *Acts: Catching Up with the Spirit* DVD, watch the video segment for Session 2 prior to the session. Prepare a question or two to be used for discussion.

- Decide when the participants will view the video during this session, whether at the beginning of the session, before or after a discussion time, or toward the end of the session. Allow 15 minutes to watch and discuss the video.

- Prepare the means to show the video to the group.

SESSION 2 OPENING DISCUSSION

Welcome the participants, especially any who are attending their first session. Ask participants who were present for the previous session to talk briefly about an insight or a question from it that "stuck with them" through the week, and whether they said or did anything specific to be a witness for Jesus. Be ready to talk about your own answers to these questions.

Ask participants to think about a situation in which they were a stranger or an outsider. Invite volunteers to discuss these questions:

- What, specifically, did you think and feel as an outsider in this situation?
- If you became an insider instead of an outsider, how did that change happen? If you did not, why not?
- How has this experience influenced the way you relate to outsiders in situations where you are already an insider? Again, be ready to start discussion by talking about such an experience you have had.

Tell participants that in *Acts: Catching Up with the Spirit*, chapter 2, Matthew Skinner explores stories in Acts about "insiders" and "outsiders" in the early church, and how these stories can instruct Christian communities today.

OPENING PRAYER

Saving and surprising God, you led your Son's earliest followers to new understandings of and responses to the expansive reach of your grace. Through this session, may your Holy Spirit startle us with fresh and freeing insights into your love not only for us but also for others; and so fill our minds and hearts that we imagine new

*ways to reach out to those whom you have already
included in the company of Jesus Christ, who is
Lord of all. Amen.*

BIBLE READING AND DISCUSSION

Ask participants what they think of when they hear the phrase "conversion story," and write their responses on large sheets of paper or markerboard. Encourage participants to keep these responses in mind as, together, your group reads and reflects on three "conversion stories" from Acts.

Recruit volunteers to read aloud each of the following Scriptures. After each reading, use the questions provided to prompt discussion. (If time is limited, choose before your session which Scriptures your group will study.)

Acts 8:26-40

- Skinner writes that "if anyone in Acts represents the concept of *outsider*," the Ethiopian official in this story does. Why? (You might want participants to consult these other Bible verses for background: **Deuteronomy 23:1** (a restriction on who belonged to the community of God's people); **Numbers 12:1** ("Ethiopia" is called "Cush" in some translations); **Jeremiah 38:7-13** (an Old Testament story of another Ethiopian eunuch who serves a ruler); **Psalm 68:28-31** (a prayer for God to show God's power).

- Despite being an outsider in several ways, the court official, notes Skinner, "may be Jewish or well acquainted with Judaism since he has been to the Temple and is reading a prophetic book." When have you been surprised to discover that you share something in common with a stranger or

21

outsider? How did this common ground affect your relationship with this person?

- The Ethiopian says he needs someone to help him understand the Scripture. When have you needed another person to guide you as you read Scripture? What do we gain from reading Scripture with other people that we cannot gain when we read it by ourselves?

- Why might the eunuch identify with the person described in the Scripture he is reading (**Isaiah 53:7-8**)? Which Scriptures, if any, lead you to identify in some way with Jesus—and which Scriptures lead you to identify those people you regard as strangers or outsiders with Jesus?

- Why do you think this story doesn't include a detailed record of what Philip said to the Ethiopian eunuch?

- Skinner relates how he has discovered that this story is important "for people who have been denied power, dignity, and a place at the table in Christian history." How is this story good news for such people?

Acts 9:1-20

- "What happens to Saul is one of the most famous stories in Acts," writes Skinner. Why do you think this is so? Why is what happens to Ananias in this story arguably far less famous?

- Skinner points out that, like many prophets in Scripture, Ananias "is minding his own business when the Lord calls him to perform a task," and "offers reasons why it's a bad idea." (Compare, for example, **Exodus 4:1-17**; **Isaiah 6:1-11**; **Jeremiah 1:4-10**.) Why is initial resistance to God's call so often the mark of a true prophet? What risks does Ananias run by agreeing to go to Straight Street to heal Saul?

- Why is Ananias's addressing Saul as "brother" significant? When, if ever, have you recognized someone you initially regarded as a stranger, outsider, or even an enemy as a fellow member of God's family? How easy or difficult did that recognition come, and what happened as a result?

- "It's easier to talk about the new possibilities the good news brings," writes Skinner, "than it is to live into them wholeheartedly like Ananias does." When have you seen Christians, individually or as a group, embracing God's "new possibilities"? How did others respond?

Acts 10:9-16, 25-36, 42-48

- How does the vision that Peter sees prepare him for his visit to Cornelius, "a centurion of the Italian Cohort" (Acts 10:1) and a Gentile (non-Jew)?

- How does Cornelius's vision of "a man in radiant clothing" (verse 30 CEB) prepare him for Peter's visit to him?

- Have you ever had a visionary experience, as Peter and Cornelius did? If so, what was it like, and do you believe it was from God? If not, do you believe God still communicates through visions, as recorded in Scripture? What criteria should the church use to discern which visions contain authentic messages from God?

- The man in Cornelius's vision tells Cornelius that God has heard Cornelius's prayers and seen his "compassionate acts" (verse 31 CEB). How much or how little would taking seriously the idea that God hears all people's prayers shape the way you pray?

- Do you think God's notice of those who do "what is right" (verse 35) extends even to those who profess no faith? Why or why not?

- Peter baptizes Cornelius and his household because they "have received the Holy Spirit just as [Jewish followers of Jesus] have" (verse 47). How can Christians recognize the Spirit's presence and activity among groups of strangers and outsiders today, and how should they respond?

- "Long-standing boundaries that Peter had internalized since his childhood," writes Skinner, "are suddenly no longer in force." What boundaries between and distinctions among people has your faith led you to reevaluate? What conclusions about these boundaries and distinctions have you reached, and why?

- Skinner states "the basic belief set down in this story is that there are no qualitative differences among various kinds of Christians. No one group enjoys an inherent advantage over another. The church doesn't have a minor league team or a remedial class." In your experience, how well does the church—in general, and in your congregation—reflect this basic belief in its practice? When have you seen it honor this conviction, and when have you seen this conviction contradicted?

After your group has read and discussed the Scriptures, invite them to look back at the list of what participants think about "conversion stories." Ask: How do these stories from Acts confirm or challenge what you think about "conversion"?

PLAN TO TAKE ACTION

Matthew Skinner argues the "conversions" in these stories involve the church changing as much as the "converts." He writes, "The church in Acts . . . repeatedly discover[s] that the good news has consequences, including the radical embrace of other people. Acts encourages us to look for opportunities to welcome, include, and commit ourselves to others not as polite things to do but as moments of divine revelation." Ask and discuss:

- Who are the people outside our faith community God wants us to welcome, include, and commit ourselves to?

- What are some specific and practical ways we as a faith community could do (or are currently doing) that?

- Who are the "strangers" in your own life God is calling you, personally, to welcome?

CLOSING PRAYER

Lord Jesus, when you hung on your cross, you stretched your arms wide and embraced us. May we open our arms and hearts always wider to embrace more of the people you also love, ready to be changed so we live ever more faithfully as your witnesses. Amen.

Session 3

DISCERNMENT AND CHANGE

SESSION OBJECTIVES

This session's Bible readings, discussion, reflection, and prayer will equip participants to

- reflect on experiences making decisions as part of secular groups and as part of the community of faith;

- explore similarities and differences between "decision" and "discernment";

- examine stories from Acts about how the early church made decisions for insights that can help the church discern God's will and make decisions today; and

- consider their congregation's budget as a concrete example of their church's decision making and discernment.

VIDEO SEGMENT

- On the *Acts: Catching Up with the Spirit* DVD, watch the video segment for Session 3 prior to the session. Prepare a question or two to be used for discussion.

- Decide when the participants will view the video during this session, whether at the beginning of the session, before or after a discussion time, or toward the end of the session. Allow 15 minutes to watch and discuss the video.

- Prepare the means to show the video to the group.

SESSION 3 OPENING DISCUSSION

Welcome the participants, especially any who are attending their first session. Ask participants who were present for the previous session to talk briefly about an insight or a question from it that "stuck with them" through the week, and how they showed welcome to "strangers" in their lives and communities. Be ready to talk about your own answers to these questions.

Invite participants to think about a time when they have been part of a group *other than* a church or faith community that was trying to make a decision. Ask volunteers to respond to these questions:

- What was the decision that had to be made?
- What specific steps did the group take to reach a decision?
- What specific steps did the group *not* take that you think it should have taken, and why?
- How confident did the group feel about the decision it reached?

Ask all participants:

- How much more difficult is group decision-making than personal decision-making, and why?
- In your experience, how differently do churches make decisions than other groups do?
- How differently do you think churches *should* make decisions? Why?

Tell participants that in *Acts: Catching Up with the Spirit*, chapter 3, Matthew Skinner examines stories from Acts about some important decisions the early church made. Read aloud this passage from Skinner's book:

Acts is a helpful book for decision-making congregations to consider—not because it tells us exactly how to make decisions but because it understands the weight a decision can hold for Christians' common life.

OPENING PRAYER

Eternal God, who founded the world by wisdom and whose Holy Spirit still calls all people to get knowledge and gain insight: Grant us clear minds and open hearts to seek your instruction and guidance in this time together, that we may learn from believers in the past how to think about the decisions we must make in the present as followers of Jesus Christ, who became for us wisdom from you, and righteousness, holiness, and deliverance. Amen.

BIBLE READING AND DISCUSSION

Write two words on the large sheet of paper or markerboard: DECISION and DISCERNMENT. Ask: "How are 'decision' and 'discernment' like and unlike?" Write participants' responses.

Tell participants that this session's stories help clarify the relationships and differences between decision and discernment in the early church's experience and can offer us models for thinking about decisions we have to make as Jesus' church today.

Read aloud from *Acts: Catching Up with the Spirit*:

What happens in Acts is less about choosing and deciding and more about discerning. When I speak of discernment, I mean a process that involves reflection on who God is, what God desires, and how we—God's people—might play a part in being faithful to God's purposes. Discernment entails more than just collecting data, making projections, and choosing a sensible course of action. Discernment is an act of faith, because in the end the discerners don't say, "This is what we choose" but "This is where we think we will discover the challenges and rewards of faithfully bearing witness to Jesus."

Have participants turn to Acts 6. Recruit a volunteer to read aloud **Acts 6:1-6**.

Acts 6:1-6

- What problem faces the church in this story? (See **Acts 2:44-46; 4:34-35** for some context.)

- According to Matthew Skinner, the story describes "grumbling" among the believers and he notes, "Anyone who works with groups knows that grumbling can produce resentment and hostility, which is where especially damaging troubles live." When have you experienced "grumbling" in groups, including churches, you've been a part of? What happened because of it and how, if at all, did the group deal with it?

- Skinner writes that "stated and unstated values always guide a church's decision-making, and there are always theological implications to the values we choose to employ." What stated and unstated values do you find in the early church's solution for this problem? Which of these values do you share and affirm, and why? Which ones do you have questions about or do you object to, and why?

- For Skinner, this story highlights the church's need to change its procedures when they fail to accomplish God's mission: "Not all procedures are meant to last forever, especially if they prove discriminatory in ways that run counter to the good news." When, if ever, has your church changed its procedures in order to more faithfully follow Jesus? How easy or difficult was the change, and what helped your church accomplish it?

- What procedures, if any, do you think your church still needs to change in order to more faithfully and effectively witness to Jesus?

Tell participants that, in chapter 3 of *Acts: Catching Up with the Spirit*, Skinner next discusses how Peter explains his baptism of Cornelius and other Gentiles, which your group studied in the last session, to the rest of the church in Jerusalem (**Acts 11:1-18**). Tell them Skinner states the inclusion of Gentiles "might have been the most influential development that occurred during the church's first generation," and that the next story your group will read further explores the impact of that decision.

Have participants turn to Acts 15. Recruit volunteers to read **Acts 15:1-21** aloud. (Consider asking one person to read Peter's words, another James's words, and a third to read as narrator.)

Acts 15:1-21

- What is the issue about Gentile Christians that causes controversy within the church in Antioch in this story? Why was this question so important? (Read **Exodus 19:1-6**; **Leviticus 19:1-2**; **Psalm 19:9-13**; and **Matthew 5:17-20** for some potentially helpful background.)

- "Some readers may be shocked to see Pharisees belonging to the church," writes Skinner. "The caricature is that all Pharisees were self-righteous, hypocritical, and opposed to Jesus' message of a gracious God. Everything about that description is a distortion. . . . There was no reason a person could not be scrupulous about his or her own Torah observance (as the Pharisees were) and a Christian at the same time." Pharisees wanted all Jews, not just priests, to observe God's Torah (literally, "instruction") in order to serve the world as a people witnessing to God's holiness. As Skinner notes, Acts doesn't preserve their arguments in these deliberations: "History is written by the winners, as they say." Why might the inclusion of Gentiles (non-Jews) in the church, then, especially concern the church's Pharisee members? What arguments do you imagine these Pharisees made?

- Paul, Barnabas, and the other believers from Antioch tell the church in Jerusalem about their flourishing ministry with Gentiles. How do the apostles and elders weigh their lived experience and their received tradition and Scripture ("the Law of Moses") when reaching their decision? When your church faces decisions, how much weight does it give to personal experience on the one hand and tradition and Scripture on the other? What are the challenges in considering both, and the dangers in not paying enough attention to either?

- When was a time you experienced Scripture surprising you or challenging what you believed about God's will for you or for the church? What, if anything, did you do as a result?

31

- Peter declares, "[W]e believe that we will be saved through the grace of the Lord Jesus, just as they will" (Acts 15:11). How can emphasizing God's grace in salvation help Christians meet the challenge Skinner writes we have faced throughout history of "express[ing] their religious connections with Jews as well as their distinctions from Jews in healthy, loving, and accurate ways"? How can the church repent of and atone for anti-Jewish attitudes and actions in its past? How can it reject such behavior in the present and guard against it in the future?

- As Skinner noted in chapter 2, truly welcoming new people into a community means the community must be open to the possibility of changing. How much openness to change do you see in the apostles and elders' decision in this story, and the way in which they reached it?

- "There is no way," writes Skinner, "of organizing a meeting or a discernment process that protects us entirely from errors or injustice." Do you agree? Why or why not? How do your church's decision-making or discernment processes attempt to minimize errors or injustice? How well do you think these processes work, and why?

- Reflecting on the decision in this story, Skinner writes, "[M]ore convincing than any theological debate across a conference table were the stories of changed lives, new friendships, increased energy given to reconciliation and compassion, and unexpected experiences of solidarity and empowerment. . . . It's the things that are life-giving that finally settle the debates." When, if ever, have you experienced this to be true in your church's discussions and debates about dealing with change?

Have participants turn to Acts 21. Recruit a volunteer to read aloud **Acts 21:1-6**. (Before the reading, you may want to explain this story comes from one of the so-called "'we' passages" in Acts. Bible scholars differ about whether these passages are Luke's own firsthand accounts, or come from sources Luke used to write Acts, or reflect rhetorical flourishes of some kind. In either case, the narrator of these passages maintains a focus on the apostle Paul and his ministry.)

Acts 21:1-6

- Why did Paul and his companions have to "tear themselves away" from the community in Ephesus? (Read **Acts 20:22-24, 36-38** for some context.) When, if ever, have you followed the Spirit even though doing so caused you grief?

- Reflecting on how the believers in Tyre object to Paul's itinerary, Matthew Skinner writes, "Both sides can't be correct—that the Spirit is simultaneously leading Paul to Jerusalem while urging the Tyrians to dissuade him—or can they?" What do you think?

- Skinner states that although Paul and the Tyrians disagree about where Paul should go, their discernment has not failed. How can discernment that doesn't lead to agreement still be the result of faithfully following Jesus?

- What lessons does the way Paul and his companions leave Tyre offer Christians today who find themselves going in different directions because of, in Skinner's words, "fundamentally different theological perspectives, each arrived at in good faith"?

After your group has read and discussed all the Scripture passages, ask if participants wish to add to or amend the group's list of the similarities and differences between "decision" and "discernment."

PLAN TO TAKE ACTION

Matthew Skinner writes,

> Every decision a church makes says something about what it understands God's desires to be, who gets to share in God's work, and exactly how a church will commit itself to the justice and reconciliation at the heart of the good news. Not every decision needs to be monumental, but no decision is purely routine.

He points to church budgets as one example:

> Because budgets dictate priorities and direct resources in some directions and not others, budgets are also moral documents. If they're moral documents, they are theological documents, too.

Distribute copies of your congregation's annual budget (if available). Lead a discussion of it using some or all of these questions:

- What kind of decision-making or discernment process does our church use to set the budget?

- What does this budget say—by what it includes and by what it leaves out—about how our church understands who God is and what God wills?

- If an outsider to our church were to look at this budget, would that person see our understanding of God's will the same way we do? Why or why not?

You may want to remind participants that this exercise is not meant to criticize or attack church leaders who have prepared the budget. Instead, it is meant to help us think about how "no decision is purely routine" in the church's life.

Challenge participants to take time this week to look at their personal or household budgets with a similarly discerning eye. What do their budgets say about what they value, who they believe God to be, and how they are participating in God's work in the world?

CLOSING PRAYER

Lord Jesus, you did not promise your followers would always agree, but you promised you will always be with us, and you sent your Spirit to guide us into your truth. May we always seek to do your will and to honor you in all our decisions. Accept our actions as humble and imperfect offerings through which, only by your grace, the world may see you at work, to the glory of God. Amen.

Session 4

OPPOSITION

SESSION OBJECTIVES

This session's Bible readings, discussion, reflection, and prayer will equip participants to

- reflect on and talk about ways resistance to the church's belief and mission can strengthen the church;

- explore stories of opposition to the church in Acts and discover how they remain relevant for Christians today; and

- plan concrete actions they can take to deal with impediments to faithful witness to Jesus.

VIDEO SEGMENT

- On the *Acts: Catching Up with the Spirit* DVD, watch the video segment for Session 4 prior to the session. Prepare a question or two to be used for discussion.

- Decide when the participants will view the video during this session, whether at the beginning of the session, before or after a discussion time, or toward the end of the session. Allow 15 minutes to watch and discuss the video.

- Prepare the means to show the video to the group.

SESSION 4 OPENING DISCUSSION

Special Preparation for Leader: You will need a small piece of equipment designed for resistance strength training (for example, stress ball, dumbbell, resistance band, small bag weighted with a few books or canned goods).

Welcome the participants, especially any who are attending their first session. Ask participants who were present for the previous session to talk briefly about an insight or a question from it that "stuck with them" and how, if at all, the session influenced the decisions they made during the week. Ask any volunteers who took up the challenge of reevaluating their own personal or household budgets as a moral and theological "document" to discuss what they discovered. As always, be ready to talk about your own answers to these questions.

Demonstrate squeezing the stress ball, lifting the dumbbell, or using the other small piece of equipment designed for resistance exercises. Pass the equipment around the group, encouraging each participant to take a few turns using it. Explain that activities like this one strengthen muscles by making them work against external resistance.

Discuss:

- What other examples of resistance strength training can you think of?

- What are some external sources of resistance to the church? What are some internal sources?

- How, specifically, can resistance or opposition make the body of Christ stronger, as resistance exercises can make our physical bodies stronger?

Tell participants that in *Acts: Catching Up with the Spirit,* chapter 4, Matthew Skinner examines stories from Acts about times the early church encountered resistance and opposition.

Read aloud this excerpt from Skinner's book:

> Sometimes opposition drives us to understand
> ourselves better. . . . [W]e might clarify and
> recommit ourselves to who we are, what we
> stand for, and what we want. The result might
> be a sharper understanding of our identity and
> values.

OPENING PRAYER

Sovereign God, whose messengers met and often
still meet with disbelief and danger, and whose
Son was subjected to death on a cross: Your world
does not always welcome your will and your ways.
As we explore times of conflict and opposition
in the church's past, may your Spirit teach us
how to remain faithful in the face of resistance
today, that we might offer ever clearer and more
consistent witness to Jesus Christ. Amen.

BIBLE READING AND DISCUSSION

Have participants turn in their Bibles to Acts 1. Recruit a
volunteer to read aloud **Acts 1:15-20**.

Acts 1:15-20

- Like so many Christians, past and present, Peter
  seems struck by the fact that Judas betrayed Jesus
  even though Judas was one of Jesus' chosen apostles.
  Matthew Skinner summarizes several different inter-
  pretations of Judas's actions and motivations. What
  is your understanding of why Judas acted as he did?
  How much or how little evidence does this story,
  taken by itself, offer for that understanding?

- How is Luke's account of Judas's death like and unlike the account in **Matthew 27:3-10**? How do you make sense of these similarities and differences? How much do you think they matter, and why?

- Skinner writes, "In Luke, as well as in Acts, Judas is Satan's agent." (See **Luke 22:3**.) Although this story does not explicitly mention Satan, what "satanic influence," in Skinner's words, does it portray? How does this influence oppose the church's well-being and continued ministry? (Compare **Acts 4:32-35**.)

- "I confess I get uneasy with Christians who place too much focus on satanic power," writes Skinner. "Attributing all [wickedness] to 'Satan' sounds too convenient and hasty to overlook the evil that humanity generates all on its own." How much do you agree or disagree? How can talking about satanic influence and power help or harm the church today?

- Skinner writes, "The church, according to Acts, in its common life embodies the liberation God provides from spiritual oppression." When have you seen or experienced the church demonstrating this liberation from Judas-like greed and self-protectionism? What practical steps does or can the church take to encourage the "self-giving generosity" Skinner notes defining the church's life together in Acts?

Have participants turn to Acts 5. Recruit volunteers to read **Acts 5:17-42** aloud. (You could divide the reading as follows: verses 17-26, verses 27-33, verses 34-42).

Acts 5:17-42

- Matthew Skinner notes the purpose of the angel who frees the apostles from prison "is not to allow a clean getaway; it is to escalate the conflict." How can and do Christians today tell the difference between conflicts that are worth "escalating," if any, and those that aren't?

* Peter declares he and the apostles "must obey God rather than humans!" (verse 29 CEB). Have you or Christians you know or know of ever resisted or defied human authority because of faith? What happened?

* Summarize Gamaliel's argument against persecuting the apostles (verses 34-39). Skinner writes that, from Luke's perspective, Gamaliel's argument "actually functions to incriminate himself and the rest of the council." How do you judge Gamaliel's position and recommendation, and why?

* Have you ever wondered whether you or your church are on the wrong side of a conflict and might be found "fighting God" (verse 39 CEB)? What caused your doubts, and how did you deal with them? What happened? What criteria do you think Christians should use to discern when a "plan or activity is of human origin" or divine (verse 38 CEB)?

* Skinner writes that Acts characterizes the high priest and the council as "equally violent and unperceptive—a dangerous combination." Where else in history and/or in the present do you see this pattern of "intimidation by authorities who believe they won't be held accountable"? When, if ever, does the church have an obligation, as part of its witness to Jesus, to oppose such intimidation on others' behalf?

* Skinner writes that Acts "unhelpfully distorts the wide range of attitudes that Jews had toward (and

within) the church during the first century." Why do Christians need to acknowledge these distortions when reading Acts today?

Have participants turn to Acts 8. Recruit volunteers to read **Acts 8:9-24** aloud (perhaps reading the roles of the narrator, Peter, and Simon).

Acts 8:9-24

- First-century Jews and Samaritans had a long history of mutual mistrust and prejudice. (See **Luke 10:10-35; 17:11-19**; and **John 4:9** for New Testament evidence of this conflict.) How does Philip's evangelistic success in Samaria not only fulfill Jesus' words in **Acts 1:8** but also challenge the early church's ideas of who its enemies are?

- Skinner points out Acts' original Greek text does not draw the distinction many English translations draw between Philip's "miracles" and Simon's "magic." How do Philip's and Simon's motivations for their deeds of power distinguish them from each other? How does this distinction help Christians think about using power and influence today?

- Why does Peter react so strongly to Simon's request? When, if ever, have you known or known about people who want to "buy God's gift with money" (Acts 8:20 CEB)?

- Skinner says the story of Simon the magician serves as a warning that "corruption inside a community can be as dangerous . . . as outright aggression coming from outside." When, if ever, have you experienced the truth of this statement? What happened? What conditions allow corruption to take hold and grow within a community of faith, and how are these conditions best handled?

- "Following Jesus and honoring his teachings," writes Skinner, "usually entail unlearning other values and patterns." What values and patterns have you unlearned in your own life as Jesus' follower? Which ones do you think you still need to unlearn to follow him more faithfully?

Have participants turn to Acts 25. Recruit volunteers to read aloud **Acts 25:1-12**. Before the reading, tell participants that Festus was Rome's newly appointed governor of Judea (the same office Pontius Pilate held during Jesus' lifetime).

Acts 25:1-12

- In this story, Paul faces opposition from two sources: leaders from his own religion and an official from the occupying military power. How does Paul take and make opportunities to be a witness for Jesus even in opposition?

- Skinner writes, "Acts is not very interested in settling the question of Paul's guilt or innocence according to the outlook of Roman law and privilege." When do you think Christians need to value their fidelity to Christ more than guilt or innocence by their society's standards?

- When, if ever, have you turned opposition into an opportunity to be Jesus' witness? What happened?

PLAN TO TAKE ACTION

Read aloud from Matthew Skinner:

I'm not going to conclude this exploration of

opposition by asking you to name the church's enemies today. . . . Nor do I want to equate all "opposition" with "enemies.". . . I believe a more appropriate question than "Who is the enemy?" is "How should believers respond faithfully and responsibly to whatever impedes their ability to live out the generosity and hospitality of the good news?"

Invite participants to brainstorm with you a list of impediments or "roadblocks" they believe stand in the way of your congregation's bearing more effective witness to Jesus, using Skinner's proposed question as a guide. What obstacles would need to be cleared in order for your congregation to show people beyond its borders the love of God in Christ? Participants might identify such impediments as physical location, lack of resources, competing priorities, lack of planning— perhaps even people, although you will want to help your group avoid judgmentally dismissing others. Write responses on the large sheets of paper or markerboard.

Once the group has completed a list of several items, ask:

- Which of these impediments could we most constructively deal with in the short term?

- What are one or two concrete steps we can take now to address this impediment?

Be sure to assign follow-up responsibilities as appropriate. This activity's goal is not "solving a problem" but encouraging participants to take specific action toward more faithful witness.

Special Instructions: Encourage participants to bring with them to the next session a photograph of a person they consider a "saint" among their friends or family, defining that term however they choose.

CLOSING PRAYER

Your call, O Christ, is not always easy to answer. By your Holy Spirit, keep us focused on your faithfulness to us that we may grow stronger in our faithfulness to you. Guard us from hatred and bitterness, and fill us with ever increasing love for you and the world for which you died and were raised, by the power of God—the same power at work, by grace, within us. Amen.

Session 5

SAINTS AROUND THE EDGES

SESSION OBJECTIVES

This session's Bible readings, discussion, reflection, and prayer will equip participants to

- identify the "saints" among their friends or families and talk about these individuals' importance to them;

- explore the lives and ministries of several "supporting characters" in the Book of Acts, and extrapolate from their stories insights into faithful discipleship for today; and

- reflect on how their congregation most often chooses to tell its story, and consider ways to encourage fresh tellings in order to gain new understanding of God's work.

VIDEO SEGMENT

- On the *Acts: Catching Up with the Spirit* DVD, watch the video segment for Session 5 prior to the session. Prepare a question or two to be used for discussion.

- Decide when the participants will view the video during this session, whether at the beginning of the session, before or after a discussion time, or toward the end of the session. Allow 15 minutes to watch and discuss the video.

- Prepare the means to show the video to the group.

SESSION 5 OPENING DISCUSSION

Welcome the participants, especially any who are attending their first session. Ask participants who were present for the previous session to talk briefly about an insight or a question from it that "stuck with them" and how, if at all, the session influenced the way they reacted to any opposition they encountered when speaking or acting as witnesses to Jesus.

Invite participants who brought a photo of a "saint" (or who may have access to one via smartphone) to show and talk about it to the group. (You should be prepared to "show and tell" a photo of your own.) Who is the person in the picture? Why is the person important to the participant and the participant's family? What makes them a "saint" to the participant?

After allowing sufficient time for sharing, tell participants that this session will introduce them to some of the "saints around the edges" of the early church whom Matthew Skinner discusses in chapter 5. Read this passage from *Acts: Catching Up with the Spirit*:

> The people who operate at the fringes of the plot [of Acts] may not receive as much attention as Peter and Paul, but they are equally important to our understanding of what the first generations of believers did to help build the new society that God's Spirit was creating among them.

OPENING PRAYER

God of the ages, always you call women and men, young and old, to witness to your Son and live out your truth. May your Holy Spirit guide our reading, reflection, and discussion today, that we may find, in the stories of believers from long ago, insights to guide us as faithful followers of Jesus Christ today. Amen.

BIBLE READING AND DISCUSSION

Special Preparation for Leader: You will need to obtain Bible reference books that the groups may use in their assignments on Stephen, Tabitha (Dorcas), Barnabas, Rhoda, and Priscilla and Aquila.

Form five small groups of participants (if group size permits) and assign each group one of the following "saints around the edges" whom Skinner discusses in chapter 5. Write the names of the "saints" and the associated Bible citations on large sheets of paper or markerboard for ease of reference. Give groups about 10–15 minutes (adjust as your allotted time demands) to find out as much about their assigned "saint" as they can. As groups work, you may want to share some or all of the discussion questions printed below to help spur discussion. Tell each group that they want to "get to know" their assigned "saint" as fully as possible in the available time. Encourage them to go beyond these passages with the help of the Bible reference books you have made available. Some group members with smartphones may even choose to consult online concordances or trusted websites.

Group 1—Stephen
Acts 6:8-15; 7:54-60

- Why do you think Luke says Stephen performed "great wonders and signs" (**Acts 6:8**) without specifying what they were?

- Stephen was the church's first martyr. The word *martyr* derives from the Greek word for "witness." Stephen was also one of the church's first deacons (**Acts 6:5**). The word *deacon* (although not used by Luke in Acts 6) derives from the Greek word for "service." What connections can you make between service and martyrdom?

- Skinner notes that Stephen gives the longest speech in Acts. Read or skim Stephen's speech in **Acts 7:2-53**. What are its main themes and points? How would you describe its tone? What, if anything, about his speech surprises or troubles you? What does Stephen's speech reveal about him and his faith?

- Compare Luke's account of Stephen's arrest, trial, and death to Luke's account of Jesus' suffering (especially in **Luke 22:66–23:5** and **23:34, 44-47**). Why does Luke present Stephen's experience in ways that mirror Jesus' experience?

- Skinner states Stephen "establishes a pattern for what all disciples can expect." How, if at all, has your life followed that pattern?

- While Christians in the United States are free to worship and serve Christ, persecution and martyrdom persist in the church worldwide. What do you know about Christian martyrs elsewhere? (You may wish to look at such websites as The Voice of the Martyrs, https://www.persecution.com/). How do these modern-day martyrs' experiences give you insight into Stephen's experience? How do they influence your own faith and works?

Group 2—Tabitha (Dorcas)
Acts 9:36-42

- Why do you think Luke says Tabitha performed "good works and compassionate acts" (verse 36 CEB) without specifying what they were?

- Skinner infers from Luke's mention of this woman's two names—Tabitha (Aramaic) and Dorcas (Greek)—that she was a "bridge builder" in her diverse community. Who builds bridges of connection and understanding between different people in your faith community? in your larger community? How do you work to build such bridges yourself? How important is this bridge-building activity as part of the church's witness to Jesus?

- Skinner calls the clothes Tabitha made "an intimate and caring gift" because they require personal, attentive knowledge of the recipient. When have you received that kind of gift from someone? When have you given that kind of gift?

- Skinner writes, "Bringing [Tabitha] back to life validates the urgency of her work," which is providing the "leadership and material sustenance . . . that is supposed to dwell at the center of every Christian community." How does your church continue Tabitha's work today?

Group 3—Barnabas
Acts 4:36-37; 9:26-28; 11:19-26

- What encouraging actions does Barnabas take in these Scriptures?

- Commenting on Barnabas's support of Saul (Paul), Skinner writes, "Barnabas sees the gifts that someone else possesses and makes sure they get used. . . . People like him always change the church's story." To whom in your congregation (or another congregation or community you've been part of) could these words also apply?

- When have you seen another community member's gifts and potential and done something to encourage their use? What happened? How and when has someone done so for you?

- Like Tabitha, Barnabas builds bridges—in Acts 11, between Jews and non-Jews. Skinner notes Barnabas "would be invaluable to the attempts to keep the different kinds of believers . . . unified in their new existence as Christians." Whom have you known or whom do you know of who has special gifts for promoting Christian unity? How have you been involved in attempts to keep different kinds of believers united?

- Luke calls Barnabas "a good man" (**Acts 11:24**). In **Luke 18:19** (CEB), Luke recorded Jesus asking, "Why do you call me good? No one is good except the one God." How do we recognize goodness in others? What does it mean to call a Christian a good person?

- Likewise, what does it mean for a Christian to be "endowed with exceptional faith," and what criteria do (or ought) we use to recognize such believers?

Group 4—Rhoda
Acts 12:5-17

- Why do you imagine Peter doesn't fully realize what is happening to him as he is freed from prison? Why don't most of the people in Mary's house immediately realize what has happened, either?

- Skinner writes about a colleague who sees Rhoda as a "comedic figure" in this story. What is your opinion of Rhoda?

- How is Rhoda like the women who first testified to Jesus' resurrection (**Luke 24:9-11, 22-24**)? What conclusions, if any, might Luke want readers to reach by drawing the parallels?

- Skinner points out Rhoda was a slave (the Greek word describing her, *paidiskē*, is the same word with which Paul describes Hagar "the slave woman" in Galatians 4). "Rhoda's story," he writes, "reminds us not to idealize the early church." Do you agree that we modern Christians tend to idealize our forebears in faith? Why or why not? How do such Scriptures as **Galatians 3:26-29** and **1 Peter 2:18-22** shape our view of Rhoda's position and early church practice?

- Skinner praises Rhoda for taking her testimony and herself seriously: "She knows what she has seen and heard, and she won't waver in declaring it until everyone else finally comes to know what she knows." When have you shared Rhoda's determination to testify to what you know, and when have others been like Rhoda to you?

- Skinner states Rhoda "shows herself more willing to discover the power of prayer than anyone else." How powerful do you believe prayer is? In general, do you approach prayer more like Rhoda, or more like those who doubt her report? Why? How, if at all, would you like your attitude toward prayer to change? How could your community help?

Group 5—Priscilla and Aquila
Acts 18:1-4, 24-27

- Skinner calls Priscilla and Aquila "a power couple in the early church." Have you known "power couples" in the churches with which you've been involved? Who were or are they, and why do you consider them powerful?

- Like Paul, Priscilla and Aquila "possessed the financial means and social expertise to be mobile" and spread the good news in many places. How does this Scripture support that statement? What fiscal resources and social connections, if any, have helped you be a witness to Jesus? What resources and connections does your church use to witness to and serve Jesus?

- Skinner notes that in Acts' second half, Luke names Priscilla before Aquila, probably indicating either "that she was the more prominent or gifted of the two or that she occupied a higher social stratum than her husband." How does Priscilla challenge ancient and modern ideas about women's roles in the church and at home?

- Priscilla and Aquila instruct Apollos more fully and accurately in his faith. When and how have your fellow believers helped you more clearly understand and follow God's way? Have you ever had occasion to teach faith "more accurately" to other Christians? How did that experience affect your own faith?

When the small groups are finished with their Bible studies, ask each group to appoint a spokesperson to take part in a panel discussion. The panelists are Stephen, Tabitha, Rhoda, Barnabas, and Priscilla and/or Aquila. Encourage these spokespeople to think and speak as much like the assigned "saint" as they can. The goal is not to "act," but to answer the questions as much as they think the assigned "saint" would. As moderator, use some or all of these questions to lead the panel discussion—or think of creative questions all your own:

- How did you serve Jesus and contribute to the life of the church?

- What encouraged or discouraged you most in your life with the church?

- How did your life in the church put you in contact with people who were different from you?

- What surprises you, as a first-century Christian, the most about the church in the twenty-first century?

- If you could offer only one lesson to Christians today, what would it be?

PLAN TO TAKE ACTION

As he concludes chapter 5, Matthew Skinner asks how congregations tell their stories. He identifies three prevalent ways:

- Through data—"membership figures, names of pastors, and significant stages in developing . . . real estate."

- Through community engagement—"ways in which the church and surrounding neighborhood have interacted over time . . . demographics, programs offered, and the consequences of changes in the local economy."

- Through agents of identity and mission—"how certain people and their work have inspired resilience or helped the congregation imagine new ways forward."

Skinner says all three ways have value, but the third is "most revealing" of the Holy Spirit's activity among and through the church. As a group, discuss which of the three ways your congregation uses most often to tell its story. Ask:

- Why do we, as a congregation, most often choose to tell our story in this way?

- How could our group prompt our congregation to experiment with telling its history and story in one or both of the other ways?

- When telling our story in the third way, who would we point to as the "saints" who have helped us discern who God calls us to be and what God calls us to do?

CLOSING PRAYER

For all your saints, Eternal God—those "around the edges," those "front and center," and those everywhere in between—we give you thanks. We praise you for being at work through so many different people to build up the body of Christ on earth for a common purpose. We humbly offer ourselves for your work, as well, that with them we may bear witness to your saving might and rejoice in your never-ending love. Amen.

Session 6

THIS CHANGES EVERYTHING

SESSION OBJECTIVES

This session's Bible readings, discussion, reflection, and prayer will equip participants to

- examine their preconceptions about whether and how the good news is public and political;

- read and explore stories from Acts about the practical, real-world implications of the early church's proclamation, and make connections to how the church is or could be influencing society today; and

- reflect on how their study of Acts as a whole has shaped their attitudes toward the early church and has inspired their own and their congregation's continuing witness to Jesus.

VIDEO SEGMENT

- On the *Acts: Catching Up with the Spirit* DVD, watch the video segment for Session 6 prior to the session. Prepare a question or two to be used for discussion.

- Decide when the participants will view the video during this session, whether at the beginning of the session, before or after a discussion time, or toward the end of the session. Allow 15 minutes to watch and discuss the video.

- Prepare the means to show the video to the group

SESSION 6 OPENING DISCUSSION

Welcome the participants, especially any who are attending their first session. Ask participants who were present for the previous session to talk briefly about an insight or a question from it that "stuck with them" and how, if at all, the session helped them think about and tell the story of their faith community in new ways during the week.

Take a poll of participants, asking them to agree, disagree, strongly agree, or strongly disagree with each of the following statements (you may want to tally and record the results on the large sheets of paper or markerboard):

- Jesus' preaching about the kingdom of God was primarily spiritual, not political.

- The good news is a challenge to the world's political and economic systems.

- People who are not Christian have no reason to feel threatened by the good news about Jesus.

- Christian faith is essentially a private matter.

- The church has an obligation to speak and act politically.

Allow volunteers to talk briefly about why they responded to one or more of these statements as they did.

Tell participants that in this session, the group will read and discuss stories from Acts in which people react, positively and negatively, to what they see as the changes demanded by the early church's witness to Jesus. Read this quotation from Matthew Skinner:

> Even if Acts rarely portrays the church's representatives as deliberate agitators, nevertheless the kingdom of God that they preach and

embody has a way of challenging the status quo and its prevalent values. Their conception of God and the good news has real implications for people's lives.

OPENING PRAYER

As we open the Book of Acts again, O God, again open us—heart and mind, strength and spirit—to the radical power of your Holy Spirit to change us and to change the world. As your Son's earliest followers were accused of turning the world upside down, may our words and our deeds put your priorities above our own and your values above our society's, that we may live as the citizens of heaven you have called us to be, active for liberty and love as we await the coming of our Savior, Jesus Christ. Amen.

BIBLE READING AND DISCUSSION

Have participants turn to Acts 14. Recruit volunteers to read aloud **Acts 14:8-18**. Encourage everyone to shout the crowd's acclamation—"The gods have taken human form and come down to visit us!" (verse 11 CEB)—in unison.

Acts 14:8-18

- Matthew Skinner finds the story of Paul and Barnabas's missionary effort in Lystra "strange and amusing," in large part because of the cultural differences between the apostles and the Lystrans. (Skinner explains that poetry about gods "disguised as human travelers" may have influenced the Lystrans' response to the wonder-working apostles.) When have cultural differences landed you in "strange and amusing" situations? How, if at all, were you able to connect with other people despite these differences?

- What unintended consequences does the miracle Paul performs have? When, if ever, have your efforts to witness to Jesus led to unintended, even "strange and amusing" consequences?

- Although Paul and Barnabas ended up in Lystra because they were fleeing for their lives (see 14:5-6), could or should they have done more to prepare for a smoother presentation of the good news there? Why or why not? How important is it for Christians today to carefully consider cultural differences when witnessing to Jesus in cultural contexts they're not familiar with?

- Skinner notes Luke is "capitalizing on familiar stereo-types" of Lystrans as ignorant and superstitious as he tells this story. How can and do such attitudes get in the way of serving Jesus as his faithful and effective witnesses?

- Skinner characterizes Paul's sermon in Lystra as "desperate" and "sentimental," but also as "an effort to meet the Lystrans where they are and to offer them a new religious perspective." What do you think of Paul's attempt to salvage the situation as a chance to preach the good news?

- "If you've ever tried to explain Christian faith to someone who has had absolutely no previous expo-sure to it," writes Skinner, "you know how difficult the task can be." Have you ever been in such a situa-tion? How did you handle it? If you never have, how *would* you?

- Skinner states, "Whenever we talk about God . . . we are rarely having just an intellectual or hypothetical discussion." What does he mean? How does the personal nature of faith present both challenges and opportunities when we attempt to share it?

Optional: Recruit volunteers to summarize and explain the good news aloud in a way they think someone with no previous exposure to it could understand. Encourage other participants to listen to each attempt and point out words, images, or ideas they think would confuse such an audience. Discuss the strengths and weaknesses of each volunteer's attempt. Stress that this activity is not as much about finding the "right" way to communicate the gospel as it is about raising our awareness of how much we may take for granted when talking about it. Ask: "What can we do to bridge the gap between our assumptions and others' lack of knowledge when we want to witness to Jesus?"

Have participants turn to Acts 16. Recruit volunteers to read aloud **Acts 16:16-39**, preferably recruiting volunteers to read individual characters' dialogue with attention to meaning and feeling. During the earthquake in verse 26, encourage participants to make loud noises (stomping feet, pounding the table, and so on)!

Acts 16:16-39

- As Skinner explains, Philippi was a Roman colony, "an offshoot of Roman society transplanted way out in Macedonia," governed by the emperor's authority and structured according to Roman norms. How much does thinking about the church as a "colony" of heaven clarify its character and purpose? In what ways might that terminology be a problem?

- Why does Paul stop the enslaved woman's shouting?
  (Compare similar incidents in **Luke 4:33-35, 41**.)
  Why do you think, as Skinner points out, Paul
  doesn't act to free the woman from her human
  masters as he frees her from the spirit possessing her,
  or invite her to join the new church in Philippi?

- The woman's masters incite mob violence by making
  anti-Jewish accusations against the apostles: "painting
  Jews as sneaky outsiders, enemies of Roman society."
  What motivates the accusation? The stereotype of the
  deceptive, disloyal Jew is common in anti-Semitism,
  past and present. When have you been aware of
  this stereotype? Why do it and its power to provoke
  violence persist? How do you challenge it when you
  encounter it?

- Skinner suggests the jailer's readiness to kill himself
  after the earthquake reveals "he's the real prisoner
  . . . serving a system that perpetuates itself through
  dominance and control over others." How do his
  later actions indicate his new belief in Jesus frees
  him from that system? What systems in your society
  "imprison" people through domination and control
  today? What practical things can or should your
  church be doing to cause "earthquakes"—or at least
  tremors—to free people from these systems?

- Why does the revelation of Paul and Silas's Roman
  citizenship alarm the Philippian authorities? How
  does their reaction further illustrate a system
  designed, as Skinner says, "to oppress the strangers
  among us and to protect our traditions and privileges
  above anything else"?

- "In our wonderfully pluralistic society," writes
  Skinner, the apostles' "triumphalist" approach "can

come across as its own kind of futile attempt to grasp for dominance." Do you agree with this characterization of Paul and Silas's actions in Philippi? Why or why not? How does our society's pluralism make our Christian witness easier? How does it make that witness more difficult?

Have participants turn to Acts 19. Recruit volunteers to read aloud **Acts 19:23-41**. Recruit volunteers to read the parts of Demetrius and the Ephesian city manager, and ask all participants to shout together "Great is Artemis of the Ephesians!" at the appropriate points (verses 28, 34).

Acts 19:23-41

- Skinner explains how devotion to Artemis (Greek goddess of hunting, nature, and chastity; named Diana in Roman mythology) was key to the size, reputation, and well-being of Ephesus. Artemis's temple and statue (perhaps fashioned from a meteorite, verse 35) "drew throngs of travelers to Ephesus" with "money to spend." What or who would you identify as the "images of Artemis" on which communities today, including your own, depend for status, influence, and wealth?

- Skinner summarizes Demetrius's objection to the apostles' mission in Ephesus: "Christians won't just believe differently than they used to. They'll use money differently. If they win the battle of ideas, their values will make our values look bad. Unpopular values quickly become unprofitable." How do you spend money differently—than other people, or than you did at other points in your life—because you are a Christian?

- What ways of making money do you believe the good news threatens, as it threatened the Ephesian artisans' trade?

- Skinner asks groups studying this story, "[W]hat should the church's resisters be worried about in your neighborhood right now?" In what specific ways and to what extent does or should your church put the gospel's challenge to the status quo—"life as usual"—at the forefront of your ministries?

- A level-headed Ephesian official manages to get the rioting crowd at the amphitheater to disperse. Although this town clerk is not a Christian, does he offer Christians any insights or lessons into how we should speak and act when others resist or reject our witness to Jesus? Why or why not?

- "Christians don't all need to support the exact same causes or take up identical positions on all political issues," writes Skinner. "But commitment to Jesus Christ is supposed to influence how we live in the world." What positions do you hold, causes do you support, and actions do you take *outside* of the church that you do at least in large part *because* of your faith? When have you and other Christians disagreed about these positions, causes, and actions, and how have you dealt with those disagreements?

- As Skinner points out, Luke and his fellow first-century Christians could not have imagined the church would ever have widespread political influence and power. How should this realization shape the way Christians exercise their rights and freedom in a modern democratic society?

FINAL DISCUSSION

Skinner writes, "The Christian message and Christian living . . . have the potential to change everything. That dynamic of Acts is one of the most powerful ways that the book urges its readers to dream big and expect more from their commitment to God." Now that your group has finished this study of Acts, invite participants to think back over the sessions they've attended. Ask:

- How has this study of Acts changed your perceptions of and beliefs about the early church?

- What new questions about the early church do you have? How will you find answers?

- How has this study helped you perceive the Holy Spirit's continuing presence and activity in the life and work of your congregation? in your own life?

- What big dreams do you have for your congregation's witness to Jesus as a result of this study?

Thank all group members for their participation in the study, and express your gratitude for having had the chance to lead it.

CLOSING PRAYER

Spirit of God, you continue to blow through the world unhindered, always leading us to new experiences of your freedom, your power, and your love. Keep us faithful in following after you, knowing we pursue you only because you have first pursued us, and trusting you to draw others, through our witness, to the people you have formed for yourself in Jesus Christ, our Savior. Amen.

www.ingramcontent.com/pod-product-compliance
Lightning Source LLC
Chambersburg PA
CBHW010858090426
42737CB00020B/3417